Let my people go!

Story by Penny Frank

Illustrated by Tony Morris

D1473708

THE LION
STORY BIBLE

10

TRING · BELLEVILLE · SYDNEY

Tʜe Bible tells us
how God chose the Israelites to be his
special people. He made them a
promise that he would always love
and care for them. But they must
obey him.
This story is about a leader of the
Israelites called Moses. You can find it
in your own Bible, in Exodus, chapters
2 to 12.

Copyright © 1986 Lion Publishing

Published by
Lion Publishing plc
Icknield Way, Tring, Herts, England
ISBN 0 85648 519 7
Lion Publishing Corporation
10885 Textile Road, Belleville,
Michigan 48111, USA
ISBN 0 85648 519 7
Albatross Books
PO Box 320, Sutherland, NSW 2232, Australia
ISBN 0 86760 735 X

First edition 1986

All rights reserved

Printed and bound in Hong Kong
by Mandarin Offset International (HK) Ltd

**British Library Cataloguing in
Publication Data**

Frank, Penny
    Let my people go! – (The Lion Story
Bible; 10)
    1. Moses, *Prophet* – Juvenile
literature 2. Bible stories,
English – O.T. Exodus
I. Title   II. Morris, Tony
222′.120924   BS580.M6

ISBN 0-85648-735-X

**Library of Congress Cataloging in
Publication Data**

Frank, Penny.
Let my people go!
(The Lion Story Bible; 10)
Summary: Retells the story of the
Israelite leader Moses, as found in
Exodus.
1. Moses (Biblical leader) – Juvenile
literature.
2. Bible. O.T. – Biography – Juvenile
literature.
[1. Moses (Biblical leader). 2. Bible
stories – O.T.]
I. Morris, Tony, ill. II. Title. III. Series
Frank, Penny. Lion Story Bible; 10.
BS580.M6F66 1986   222′.1209505
85-13119
ISBN 0-85648-735-X

Moses lived in the palace of the king of Egypt. He had everything he could wish for. But he was not an Egyptian — he was an Israelite.

The other Israelites were slaves. They had to work very hard, making bricks all day in the hot sun. If they stopped, they were whipped.

One day Moses saw an Egyptian being
very cruel to an Israelite. He was so
angry that he knocked the Egyptian
down and killed him.

Moses was afraid of what the king
would do when he found out. So he ran
away from the city, to a place where no
one knew who he was. He worked as a
shepherd.

He often thought about the Israelites,
as he looked after the sheep.

One day, as Moses watched over his sheep, he saw a bush that was on fire.

'That's funny,' he said. 'The leaves are still green, even though it is burning.'

Then he heard a voice saying, 'Be careful, Moses. This is a very special place. I am the same God who spoke to Abraham and Isaac and Jacob. I have seen how my people are suffering. You are going to lead them out of Egypt. Go and speak to the king for me.'

Moses was afraid.

'The king will never listen to me,' he said. 'He will not even believe that you have spoken to me.'

But God told Moses to take his brother Aaron with him.

Moses and Aaron went to see the king.

'We have a message from our God,' they said. 'Our God says "Let my people go!"'

'I don't know your God,' said the king. 'I will not let you go.'

And he gave orders to his men to make the Israelite slaves work even harder.

God told Moses and Aaron that he would make the king let the Israelites go.

'If you don't let us go, the river will turn to blood,' Moses said to the king.

The king would not listen. And the river turned to blood.

'I will still not let the Israelites go,' said the king.

God had promised Moses that he would lead the Israelites out of Egypt to their own land.

So Moses went to the king again and said, 'Our God says "Let my people go!"'

But the king would not listen. He was angry.

The frogs that lived by the river did not like it now. They came up into the town. They jumped all over the rooms in the palace.

When the king saw all the frogs he said, 'Tell the Israelites they can go.'

But when the frogs had gone, he changed his mind.

After the frogs, there were gnats
everywhere, biting everyone.

'The Israelites can go!' shouted the
king.

But when the gnats had gone, he
changed his mind.

God then sent swarms of flies to the land of Egypt. They were everywhere — except where the Israelites lived.

The animals which belonged to the Egyptians became sick. The Israelite animals were well.

The king kept saying, 'Yes, you can go.'
But when the flies went away and the
animals were well, he changed his mind.
'You must stay here,' he said.

Moses and Aaron told the king, 'If you don't let the Israelites go you will be covered in boils and there will be hailstorms too.'

The king did not care.

Soon the Egyptians had sore boils all
over them. Then there was a terrible
hailstorm. It beat down the plants and
hurt the people — except where the
Israelites lived.

'You can go away — now,' said the
king.

But when the boils went and the hail
stopped, the king changed his mind.

Moses told the king that God would send locusts to eat his grain. And that is what happened.

Then God said he would make the daytime as dark as night.

When these terrible things happened, the king wanted to get rid of the Israelites.

But as soon as they stopped, the king changed his mind.

Then God said to Moses, 'Tell the Israelites to get ready to go. Tell the king that tonight I am coming to Egypt. Because he has not obeyed me, the oldest child in each family will die.'

Moses told the Israelites to mark the doors of their own houses with blood from an animal. Then their oldest child would be safe.

It all happened as God said it would. All God's people were safe.

Then the king of Egypt asked Moses to take the Israelites away.

'God has given us so much trouble,' he said. 'He must want you very much.'

So God took the Israelites out of Egypt. In the daytime he led them with a special cloud. At night there was a finger of fire, so that they could not lose their way.

At last they were on their way to Canaan, the land God had promised to them.

The Lion Story Bible is made up of 52 individual stories for young readers, building up an understanding of the Bible as one story — God's story — a story for all time and all people.

The Old Testament section (numbers 1–30) tells the story of a great nation — God's chosen people, the Israelites — and God's love and care for them through good times and bad. The stories are about people who knew and trusted God. From this nation came one special person, Jesus Christ, sent by God to save all people everywhere.

The story of Moses comes from the second book of the Bible, Exodus. Number 9 in The Lion Story Bible, *The princess and the baby*, tells how God saved the life of the baby Moses and had him brought up in the palace of the king of Egypt. *Let my people go!* is about one of the greatest rescues ever.

God is completely in control of his world. He is greater and more powerful than the greatest king or leader. No human being can ever take God on and win.

God is also loving. He cares for those who are poor and oppressed and who cannot defend themselves. So he hears his people when they cry to him for help — and he comes to the rescue.

The next story in this series, number 11: *Journey to the promised land*, follows the adventures of God's people after the escape from Egypt.